*R*etirement:

Your New Adventure!

It's your choice to decide if your windshield
is bigger than your rearview mirror.

by
Bob Boylan

Author | Bob Boylan
Copy Editor | Charlie Wertheim
Book Designer | Linda Fleming

PREFACE

I'm a big believer in Simon Sinek's best-selling book *Start with WHY.*

I am a very strong Christian, and I think of Holy Spirit as my chief operating officer and strategic partner.

So, I asked my strategic partner: **WHY should I write this book?**

Holy Spirit's answer was:

"Let me bring to your remembrance, Bob, that you have been gifted to be a seed planter of ideas to creatively encourage and inspire others."

Holy Spirit also reminded me that my life from age sixty-five on has been a magnificent adventure and truly one where Holy Spirit put me in a position to use the gifts He gave me.

"Why wouldn't you continue, Bob, using those gifts and helping other people design their adventure after they are sixty-five years old?"

He continued by saying, "I've given you a magnificent adventure after sixty-five years old, and why don't you pass those ideas on as 'seeds' to others, so they can design their own adventure?"

So, **the WHY was clearly defined.**

The WHAT would be to write a book that would give a lot of thought-starters to someone designing their own adventure after their retirement.

The HOW would be to create a book that is easy to read, offering challenging questions to look past the obvious "gearing down—which is wise to do, such as downsizing your home, etc—but to also add to that the chance of "gearing up" with a list of desires and passions that you now have time to focus on.

COVID-19 is totally occupying our thinking and consuming the lion's share of our conversations. As we hear what others and ourselves are always talking about, it can become discouraging.

The purpose of this book is to plant seeds to give hope, focusing on one idea:
Your windshield is bigger than your rearview mirror.

Sometimes we can be looking "hope" right in the face and not see it. The purpose of this book is for you to *see hope in the season of your retirement.*

"The ability to register and regulate our thinking requires both imagination and rationale. This ability is the most powerful ability we have. We have control over what we think about and how we think about it." — Kirk Byron Jones

You can view designing your new adventure as a proactive effort on your part to demonstrate that you do have control over what you think about and how you'll think about looking through your windshield more than your rearview mirror.

What is my profession?

I am a seed planter of ideas to creatively encourage and inspire others.

I hope you find that some of the seeds
of ideas I've planted here
will encourage and inspire you
to create a magnificent new adventure!

Bob Boylan

INTRODUCTION

Why is there an exclamation mark at the end of the title
Your New Adventure!?

In the Broadway musical "Oklahoma!" the explanation
mark is part of the copyright.

Your new adventure is copyrighted by you. It's YOUR
adventure.

I am writing this book as the pandemic of the coronavirus
is touching the entire world. A good share of what we hear
and read every day creates fear and anxiety—more than I've
ever experienced in my lifetime.

I'm hoping that by the time you are reading this book, the
peak of the coronavirus problem has been reached and we
are well onto the downside of the curve, able to control it.

And of course, this, too, will come to an end.

However, I think the global pandemic will remain in the
forefront of our minds for the rest of our lifetimes, just like
the depression of the 1930s did for those that lived through
it. They never forgot it. It impacted how they made decisions.
It impacted their ability to dream.

But they got through it. Just as we will.

It's conceivable that the coronavirus has you focused on
fear and anxiety, and it's all you can think of.

Yet you are coming up to what you've dreamed about,

planned for, and looked forward to, for many years: retiring from your professional job and starting a new adventure.

This book hopefully will help you plan the adventure of your lifetime!

You are probably outside the fray of the pandemic and how it is impacting your financial life. I am also. We've accumulated enough assets to retire. Yes, the asset base has been reduced, but it will return like it always does.

So you have a sense of calmness because you can proceed to design and create what you've dreamed of for years. It's in your control.

This book will not deal with the financial side of retirement planning. While doing a search of books about the topic of retiring, almost all of them are focused on the financial aspect.

Of course, you will do a thorough review of your assets with your financial consultant so you are clear about that important aspect of the new adventure.

This book is totally focused on ideas to help you create your new adventure of retirement.

Someday Isle

You might think this is an island in the South Pacific. Maybe the movie South Pacific was filmed there.

But it's not. It's a figure of speech we all use. We're talking to someone and we say, "Someday I'll do such and so."

But I always kid people and say "Someday is not a date on the calendar!"

However, your "someday" is within sight. Your retirement, your "someday," is within reach. You are able to start creating what you want to do in your "someday."

You will be creating your own calendar. How's that for a fresh thought!

How you choose to fill up your calendar is up to you.

This book is a tool to help you create ideas to maximize your adventure and fill your calendar with good works, good times, and good health.

A word about doing things differently.

I'm sure you've heard the expression "going outside the box."

Going outside the box—going outside the lines, as they say—is not necessarily encouraged in most organizations. You are to stay inside the box, fulfill your job description, and always do it slightly above quota!

Of course, in your "someday" list of things you intend to do in retirement, many will be outside the box, and you can hardly wait.

There is a chapter in this book called "What if There is No Box?"

It's possible that that may be a truer picture of what you're looking at as you begin to create your new adventure.

There is no box from which you can have an idea to go outside of; there simply is no box at all.

How refreshing is that to know you can fill up your brand-new box with whatever you'd like to do?

This book is totally focused on ideas to help you create your new adventure of retirement.

Why are we creating this book, and how will it benefit us as creators?

I am using my God-given gifts to be a seed-planter of ideas to creatively encourage and inspire others.

It gives me tremendous satisfaction to use my gifts.

I feel I am being utilized in a focused manner to contribute my gifts to this significant global problem.

I believe my leadership of our team consisting of Charlie and Linda will generate the same good feelings.

I want to help restore and revitalize a person who is about to retire but who is consumed by fear and loss of hope and feels that nothing will be as they had hoped.

Someone once said, "The trouble with the future is that it is no longer like it used to be." However, you are in control of what you think about and how you think about it. And because of that truth, my friend Greg Almquist from Atlanta wrote: "What is exciting about the future is that it no longer has to be as it used to be."

You are about to retire, and you are in control of how you wish to think about retiring.

I want to help you create a fulfilling retirement

I want to help you, by planting seeds of ideas, to utilize your thinking and your creativity to design a life that could, in fact, be even more fulfilling and significant than your previous professional life.

I want to give you ideas to point you in a variety of directions.

I want you to think about ways to be helpful and supportive.

Useful and significant. Creative and productive. I want to have you focus on utilizing your abilities to help others, all the while, giving you a tremendous feeling of satisfaction and usefulness.

A feeling from your heart that you made your town, your church, your community, and your city a better place.

Five years down the road, I want you to look back on what you've accomplished, and have a warm smile, and a feeling of tremendous satisfaction.

I want you to be content knowing you've made a difference.

You are about to retire, and you are in control of how you wish to think about that.

TABLE OF CONTENTS

TABLE OF CONTENTS *continued*

TABLE OF CONTENTS *continued*

Retirement:

Your New Adventure!

Ideas to Help You See that Your Windshield
is Bigger than Your Rearview Mirror

The Windshield is Bigger than the Rearview Mirror

I love this concept.
All of our lives we've looked in the rearview mirror before we start driving. Of course, you need to do that, so you drive safely and don't back into a wall. But throughout our professional and personal lives, I believe we have looked in the rearview mirror so much that we've forgotten the concept that the windshield is so much bigger.

Don't let rearview thinking minimize the vastly larger window in front of your life.

We are built to go forward.

There is a reason the windshield is bigger than the rearview mirror. Your future matters more than your past!

When we put our car in reverse, the speedometer does not even register.

You will think of this idea next time you get in your car.

Notice that the windshield is much bigger than the rearview mirror. Hold that thought as you select colors from your palette to paint an amazing picture of your future through the windshield.

Discussion thought-starters
Select friends who are "windshield people, not rear-view-mirror people" with whom to discuss ideas.

"Windshield thinking," by definition, will create vastly larger opportunities to go forward than rearview-mirror thinking will.

Consider making two different lists:
Windshield ideas and rearview mirror ideas.

There is a reason the windshield is bigger
than the rearview mirror.
Your future matters more than your past.

How Stable is Your Tripod?

My second profession is a landscape photographer.

A good, stable, solid tripod is an absolute necessity, or I can't take good pictures.

It's not just "nice to have one" or "use it when it's convenient": It's a necessity!

Your three-legged tripod is a necessity for you also.

- Mind
- Body
- Spirit

For decades, hospitals in America have promoted "wellness programs." All wellness programs comprise the same three legs:

- Mind
- Body
- Spirit

Why do I bring this up right away?

You need to assess your "wellness" with regard to the same three legs as you create Your New Adventure!

Period. No option.

You need a three-legged tripod—not a two-legged one or a mono-pod with one leg. It doesn't work in photography, and it won't work for you.

It's a necessity for you as you plan to live out Your New Adventure!

You'll need others to help you assess the quality of your tripod.

You'll need to look deep inside to assess the quality of your tripod.

By the way, before we start, I suggest you go purchase a tripod. Get it home and label each leg: mind, body and spirit. Stand it up in your home office and look at it to see if each leg is the same length. They have to be in order to stand erect to platform the life you are creating for Your New Adventure!

Discussion thought-starters

Here are some thought-starters to get you reviewing and researching the quality of your tripod:

How stable is each leg?

How long is each leg? Is one leg much different in length?

Can you rely on it to stand tall?

What's your realistic expectation of the strength, length, and stability of each leg?

MIND

Have you been using the thinking and problem-solving opportunity-seeking part of your brain?

Have you been stretching the creative part of both logical and emotional parts of your brain and heart?

Do you have trusted financial advisors to give you solid information you can count on?

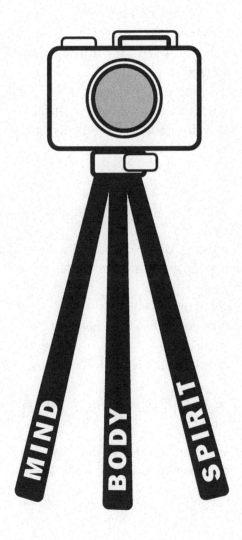

BODY

Is your health above average, average or below average?

What can you do to get your health at a higher, more stable, stronger place?

This part of the wellness program, the wellness people just love because a plethora of programs exist that you can tap into to make fairly dramatic improvements. Downright measurable progress!

SPIRIT

Are your "dreaming muscles" raring to go, or do they need some lubrication?

Do your dreaming muscles need some stimulation, like maybe a massage, to get them limbered up for Your New Adventure!?

Are you ready to dream bigger?

Do you feel like you've been "on hold" or held back in that part of your tripod?

What do you feel you're ready to "cut loose and go do?" (Just like Nike)

If you practice a faith, how strong is it supporting your actions of daily life?

It's an absolute must to start Your New Adventure! with this tripod wellness check-up!

You know this is not a fluffy idea. It's essential to have a stable tripod as you plan Your New Adventure!

You must start your new adventure
with a "tripod wellness checkup"

What Do You Want?

My profession where I have applied my seed-planting idea skill has been as a presentation trainer to middle and senior management who work for Fortune 500 companies.

I have spent thirty-eight years in front of ten-person workshops "Delivering Training that Takes."

That was my promised outcome: Delivering Training That Takes. They would be more skilled and more effective at presenting their idea of the moment!

I wrote two books about presenting that are still in the market on Amazon:

- *What's Your Point? and Stop being predictable!*

Why is this chapter titled "What Do You Want?" Because my professional background about presenting teaches that "A presentation is a recommendation!"

You must ask yourself as you are creating your presentation, "What do I want?" If you aren't clear about what you want, you will not build a strong body of evidence to support your recommendation.

And you won't get what you want.

My guess is you have all listened to those meek, mild, and usually long and boring presentations.

No one, including the presenter, gets too excited.

There is not much energy being displayed or communicated.

It's flat and lifeless. There is no "WOW!"

I am suggesting that effective planning of Your New Adventure! needs some clear answer to the question "What do you want?"

It's your opportunity to *begin to answer that question* so that you have a rough goal in mind that you see Your New Adventure! heading towards.

The majority of what comprises this book will be short chapters to expand your thinking and dreaming muscles.

I will not be writing what I believe Your New Adventure SHOULD be.

But I will be writing ideas to help you determine your answer to **"What Do You Want?"**

**The rest of this book has lots of thought-starters,
so here we go!!**

"The indispensable first step
to getting the things you want
out of life is this: **decide what you want.**"

— Brian Tracy

Most of Us Have Little Experience at "Gearing Down"

The fact of the matter is, most of us have very little experience at gearing down, or slowing down our pace.

One of the major transitions you are entering into is changing the pace of how you will lead your life.

Usually, as your responsibilities increased in your professional life, so did the pace. You cherished the energy and discipline of the pace. It was a challenge, but you embraced it. Maybe even loved it.

Now, all of a sudden, the pace—or some people say "the race" —is coming to a screeching halt.

If you really loved the pace, what new passion will generate that pace?

Knowing you can now generate whatever pace you want, what combination of activities will accomplish that?

You will need to think seriously about the best way to gear down. I'm not talking about sleeping in every morning or being a couch potato. I'm suggesting that there are options when considering the best way to gear down. Your pace becomes your decision.

Your pace becomes your decision.

Most of Us Have Learned to "Gear Up" Pretty Well

A friend of mine from the Aspen, Colorado, area, who was very fit, was talking about snowshoeing and cross-country skiing. The person said to me, "You know, Bob, I enjoy going up more than going down. It makes me feel exhilarated. I monitor my heartbeat so I know just how hard I can push. Coming back down just isn't as exciting."

It's similar to taking on a new project at work. Part of the reason, in your opinion, was the necessity to "gear up." If you didn't, you simply couldn't get the job done. That gearing up is what you've been used to. It's been part of your life. You may even have complained that it was happening too often, but down deep you loved the adrenaline rush.

Here again, it's your option how hard you wish to gear up in the next phase of your life.

You will see in this book a lot of options for gearing up to keep you mentally sharp and fully alive. I personally believe that gearing up is a necessity to leading a life that will leave the kind of legacy you want.

It's possible that you may choose to gear up and become more physically fit than you have been in the last twenty-five years. That is certainly possible, and there are many books and programs available to guide you on that path.

It's possible that you may choose to gear up and follow what's been the passion of your life but always took second place because you were so occupied with your full-time professional life.

Discussion thought-starters

What are some activities and responsibilities that you are delighted to give up in order to allow yourself to slow down your pace?

What activities can you add to your life that will give you the excitement of gearing up?

It's your choice, your chance, to actually "balance" gearing down and gearing up.

In my opinion, you will find that doing both will generate a substantially better life. It's not only my opinion; it's also a well-researched fact!

I personally believe that gearing up
is a necessity to leading a life that will
leave the kind of legacy you want.

"Have Fun, Bob!"

My mother was eighty-five, and I was visiting her in the nursing home. I knew I had one more question. We had already told each other multiple times how much we loved each other, but I still had one more question.

"Mom, you have lived an extremely productive life. What direction can you give me to lead as productive a life as you have led?"

My mother paused, understood the weight of my question as well as the honor it bestowed upon her, looked me straight in the eye, and said, "Have more fun."

She then proceeded to tell me how she had done that in her life.

Then she looked at me and said, "You're doing pretty well on that score in three areas. But, my son, your shorts are too tight!"

She explained to me through tears running down both of our cheeks what she meant. "My shorts are too tight." From my eighty-five-year-old mother. And of course, my mom was dead right.

After about fifteen minutes of what I believe is the most clear and compelling conversation I've ever had with anyone, and with tears continuing to run down my cheeks, I said, "I got it Mom; anything else?"

She shot right back, "Yes. . . . Have more fun."

I told this story to my mentor, Jim Shannon. Jim was very wise, and many people across our country sought his counsel. Jim said, after hearing this story, "That is the wisest thing I've heard in a decade."

I write this so that you may consider my mother's advice. "Have more fun."

Discussion thought-starters

What desires of your heart will generate the most fun?

What will put a smile on your face and a giggle in your heart?

What are some activities, events, and travel adventures that will provide fun?

With whom do you want to spend more time?

With whom do you want to laugh out loud?

With whom do you want to be downright silly?

In what areas of your life do you wish to take yourself less seriously?

Knowing that, do you have any habits or activities that need to change in order to have more fun?

What desires of your heart
will generate the most fun?

"Now What?" Or ... "What now?"

You have the opportunity to define your answer.

In your past life it was usual for someone else to define the next "Now what." Sometimes you were excited about that "Now what." But many times your reaction, usually said to yourself, was, "What now?" Meaning, it was not a positive reaction.

Now you have the opportunity to decide the answer to "Now what?" that generates aliveness in your being. It will be the aliveness created by designing Your New Adventure!

Discussion thought-starters

I believe now is the time to start to define your next "purpose" that will fuel your passion and help define "now what."

It's entirely possible you have never defined your purpose prior to this time.

You've always been too busy just getting your job done and raising a family. The truth is, most people have actually never defined their purpose.

The largest selling book in the history of the United States, next to the Bible, is Rick Warren's *The Purpose Driven Life*.

Richard Leider's book *The Power of Purpose* is another landmark book on the importance of defining your purpose.

What abilities, experiences, and gifts do you have?
How do you see yourself contributing those gifts?
By answering these two questions, you are well on your way to defining your purpose.
I suggest you read one or more books on the subject and then define your purpose. It will drive everything you do.
You have the opportunity to define your next "purpose." Once defined, that purpose is what will fuel your passion so that you always enthusiastically say, "Now What!"

"It does not take much strength to do things, but it requires great strength to decide on what to do."
— Elbert Hubbard

Even Eagles Need a Push

Author David McNally wrote a powerful book named *Even Eagles Need a Push*.

Baby eagles are born on the side of a cliff with no room to walk around. They are fed and cared for so they can grow up and be king of the sky.

Then one day mama eagle says, with a gentle nudge to her new child, "It's time to fly now." As the baby eagle drops downward through the sky, he must learn how to fly immediately to become what he was born to be: king of the sky.

By definition, I believe you are an eagle. You have arrived at retirement after many years of honorable and productive work. Your place in life and your finances define you as an eagle.

However, even eagles need a push. And you are being pushed into retirement. I believe you have the chance to choose between coming in for a soft landing or really taking off and flying higher than you've ever been.

Discussion thought-starters

It is time to be honest with yourself: Are you more excited about coming in for a soft landing or taking off on a new adventure?

It's obvious that each of us will do some downsizing and cutting back on the pace we no longer desire or are able to maintain. We will "gear down."

But what passions or activities get you all charged up so you feel like you are really taking off for possibly the most significant ride of your life?

You are being pushed now. Your choice: Consider coming in for a soft landing or really taking off!

"It is not by accident that the happiest people are those who make a conscious effort to live useful lives."
— Ernest A. Fitzgerald

Your Options ... Retire or Redirect

This is your call and your choice. No one else can make it for you, nor should you let anybody make it for you.

There are no designated hitters.

You can decide to retire, and your glide path is set to take you in for a soft, safe landing. It has been the conventional "picture of retirement." You may have held that picture in your mind for a long time, and that is what you choose to do. It's a good picture, perfectly normal, and will fulfill what you have dreamed about for years.

Or you could decide to redirect.

The rest of this book is about ideas to redirect. It's about ideas so that your life really takes off for quite possibly the most significant adventure of your life.

Discussion thought-starters

What is the picture you've painted in your mind for many years?

Your ability to dream new ideas does not diminish with age. What dreams might you pursue in this next adventure?

If you dig down deep in your heart, is it true that your dreaming ability has not stopped and may even be getting stronger?

Since by definition you are no longer inside of your work paradigm but can now think bigger, broader, more beautiful dreams, what are some examples of your dreams?

Could your dreams be the foundation for your new purpose?

If you decide to redirect, you will need to change gears up as well as down. Changing gears down is a necessity as we age, and there are certain things we just can't do as well as we used to.

But you will need to decide to gear up. Learn some new things, travel to some new places, and meet some new people. And above all, possibly take some new risks.

"Many of us have lived lives paralyzed by unexplored yearnings."

— Mary Morrissey

What instinctively do you already know you want to do regularly?

Don't Freeze Up Prematurely

Upon retirement, you may feel like you are clicking on all cylinders. You may feel you are at your most productive level ever. You may still be filled with energy. Your zest for doing new things seems to be at an all-time high.

Therefore, don't freeze up these skills and feelings prematurely. Realize they are in you and you simply need a new purpose on which to focus.

Discussion thought-starters

It's fairly common that you come up with a way to use your current skills at a much more reduced pace. How would you do that?

If you follow that path, how will you make sure new passions have enough time to grow and prosper?

"An instinct without execution is only a regret."

— T.D. Jakes

Discovering What Makes You Tick NOW

When I turned fifty, I just had finished delivering training in Europe, and I took a six-day break by myself and went to a small hotel outside of Innsbruck, Austria. It was called Gasthof Schwarz. I was the only American there. Sitting on a sun-drenched patio after breakfast one morning, I was planning a challenging hike.

But my mind took me to the question, "I'm about to turn fifty, and my life is extraordinary. Why is it extraordinary?"

That question jump-started me to begin writing immediately what I called "Discovering What Makes Me Tick."

I have discovered it to be an invaluable process as I look back years later to that simple question. My answers helped me realize what values make me tick and make me who I am.

Measurable progress makes us feel productive each day.

This is a major transition in your life, and it is worth sitting down all by yourself to answer the question, "What makes me tick NOW?"

"Now" is a critical word, because based on the answers you will have the foundational guidance system, your own GPS, that allows you to build a very strong future.

The foundation must be strong so that the building can grow tall. So you'll have a strong, stable, evenly balanced tripod.

Discussion thought-starters
In addition to answering the question by yourself, dialogue with others to discover if they agree with what you have written.

Other people's perceptions of you, along with what's important to you, help you clarify your guidance system.

"The big question is at your best, who are you?"

— John Ortberg

We Will All be the Same Five Years from Now

I have been saying this for a long time. People have told me they put this quote on their refrigerator. As we all know, that's where the important things of our lives go.

We will all be the same five years from now with the exception of:

- The books we read.
- The people we meet.
- The places we go.
- The risks we take.

These statements are true; they are the "gold standard" that our personal growth is based on. They are truisms.

Therefore, the obvious ways to grow in five years are to:

- Read different kinds of books
- Engage with new people, new cultures, and even new languages
- Go places you've never been
- Take more risks

Just comprehend how powerful this thought process is that you are in control of. Your former position or your profession is not in control of these things as much as it was.

Now you own these opportunities to grow.

Discussion thought-starters

Ask your friends who know you well how they have seen you function in life over the years in regard to the four ways we can change. You have the opportunity to grow in what you learn, in the people you meet, the places you go, and the risks you will take. Does that set of ideas get you all jazzed up?

Or is that just too much of a change?

"If you want to uncover your life's purpose from this point on, you must think of yourself in a new way."

— Richard Leider

You Don't Grow Old. You Get Old When You Stop Growing.

You've heard the conversations. They start out with either "Remember when we used to . . ." or "Guess what I'm planning to do next month?"

All of us have a tendency to be in one camp or the other in this regard.

You will choose the conversations you enjoy. You will choose "remember when" or "guess what I'll be doing next month."

Which conversation do you enjoy participating in? What types of conversation get you all jazzed up and feeling alive?

If we don't set our sights on growing or gearing up in some new areas of our life, we will fall into the camp of talking about "remember when."

You will choose to continue growing or stop growing. In the process, you are choosing the types of people you will surround yourself with.

I highly recommend you talk about your future instead of your past.

Discussion thought-starters

What activities, dreams, events, and adventures of all kinds get you excited?

What conversations are downright boring to you and you'd rather not engage in?

"It takes a lot of courage to show your dreams to someone else."

— Erma Bombeck

"You know you're old when you have lost all your marvels."

— Merry Browne

I highly recommend you talk about your future **instead of your past.**

Be as Good As You Think You Are

Most of us down deep think we are pretty good, maybe downright first-class.

Now you have the opportunity to be as good as you think you are.

No more built-in restrictions, patterns of predictable behavior, or new corporate initiatives to force your concentration on yet another new activity.

Now you can focus on activities that will allow you to live out a life where you can deliver the goods.

You can actually demonstrate, through your choices, the kind of person you are down deep. You can live out what makes you tick. How exciting is that?!

Discussion thought-starters

What past clutter in your busy life can now be discarded?

What will you focus on to increase your passion to be as good as you think you are?

"My whole life hasn't been written yet. I'm writing it now. I can be whatever I want to be. The present does not dictate the future."

— Mary Morrissey

Go Forward, Bob

"Say this every day, Bob. Yes, every day out loud. And you will be just fine."

My mentor, Father Arnold, gave me this extremely wise advice. He would also add a story about sitting in an automatic car wash, where the sign in front of the car wash tells you to put your car in neutral.

Father Arnold used to tell me, "I hate being in neutral. Even going in reverse is better because you are at least moving.

"Be going somewhere forward every day, Bob, because even God can't steer a parked car." I will absolutely never forget that.

I believe the point has been made.

Discussion thought-starters
What typically stalls you from moving forward?
What activities would move you forward daily?

"Be going somewhere forward every day, Bob, because even God can't steer a parked car."

What Will be Your "proclivity"?

Instinct is a book by T.D. Jakes. This author uses the word *proclivity*. It is defined as "a tendency to choose or do something regularly; an inclination or predisposition towards a particular thing."

Why don't you try to answer the question: For what will you have a proclivity during your new ride, the one that might possibly be the best ride of your life?

The book Instinct has a good chance of helping you generate trust in your instincts as you get ready for Your New Adventure!

I'll bet you know "instinctively" what "ride" you want to take—or better yet, what dream to take.

Discussion thought-starters

Are there some activities you want to stop doing?

I believe instinctively you know what activities you to want to do regularly, even almost every day. What are they?

"Instincts are your compasses guiding us from where we are to where we want to go."

— T.D. Jakes

What past clutter in your busy life
can now be discarded?

The "Gymnasium of the Mind"

Today reading is easier than ever because of products like Kindle. Today there are more electronic books sold than paper books.

If you don't have a Kindle or similar reading device, simply go get one. You are able to download free samples of a book so you can explore new authors and subjects.

What a powerful metaphor: "the gymnasium of the mind."

We need to "work out" in that gymnasium with new books to help us generate new information that will platform our instinctive dreams. Then we can act.

Therefore, go work out!

Discussion thought-starters

What do you no longer have to read?

What subjects get you excited about learning?

Is it time to invest in a Kindle?

Is it time to start using the huge resources of your local library?

"Be transformed by the renewing of your mind."

— the Apostle Paul

"Reading is the gymnasium of the mind. It is the place where thoughts are exercised and minds are stretched and challenged."

— T.D. Jakes

Your "One-liners"

Most of us have what I call "one-liners" that have been key phrases that we return to many times in our life. We return to them when making big decisions, coping with changes or problems, or considering an opportunity.

In this transition, I suggest that it is a good time for you to write out your one-liners. Realize that they have been the bedrock of how you have made decisions, taken risks, and moved forward in your life.

Regarding my own one-liners, I've discovered they are my "life's philosophy wrapped up in a few lines."

Some examples of mine:

"Give 110 percent in everything you do, always. 110 percent. Clear?"

— My dad

"You can accomplish anything you want to in your life, son, if you clearly understand the work necessary, and then be disciplined to do your work. Then, you can accomplish anything."

— My mom

"Go forward, Bob."
> — Father Arnold Weber

"To know and not do is to not know."
> — Father Arnold Weber

"Have fun, Bob."
> — My mom

"Do not lead a woulda, coulda, shoulda life."
> — Father John Powell

"Always hustle. ALWAYS. Clear?"
> — My college baseball coach

"It takes courage to be happy."
> — A friend from church

Take time to realize what your one-liners are. Discover again how much they mean to you and how powerful they are.

These one-liners will help you move in the correct direction and act with the energy, attitude, diligence and hope to help you enjoy Your New Adventure!

Discussion thought-starters

Which one-liners do you repeat most often?

Which one-liners quite frankly have become your very nature and character?

What are Your BGOs?

My book *What's Your Point?* is about how to be a more effective presenter. It was written in 1985. It's still in print and still makes sense.

In my writing and teaching style, I use the term "BGOs." It stands for Blinding Glimpses of the Obvious.

It's my style of teaching. It's my style of writing. Hopefully, some of these BGOs are helping you design Your New Adventure!

Here is a worthwhile exercise.

When you complete this book, or as you're reading it, jot down ideas that appear to be obvious suggestions. Obvious directions. Obvious processes. Obvious actions.

Now you are clearly on the way to designing the type of adventure you choose to take. You may say to yourself, "Obviously I should do this!"

Discussion thought-starters

What seems obvious so far?

After you complete the book, what additional things have you discovered that are obvious?

Discuss these obvious opportunities with your best friends to see if they think the obvious is something you should take on.

The Power of Imagination

I believe it all begins with dreaming to fuel our imagination.

Thomas Friedman, the well-published author, says in his book *The World Is Flat* that it has become obvious that America cannot competitively manufacture many of the products we dream up. "But America is still the dream capital of the world."

I say, you cannot move toward anything fulfilling if you're not dreaming.

What we dream about, we think about.
What we think about, we talk about.
What we talk about with some repetition, we act on.
What we act on repeatedly becomes a habit.
Our habits generate our character.
Our character generates our destiny.

It starts with dreaming what could be. The kind of dreaming when you dig down deep in your gut and you ask yourself the question, "Why not?"

Explosive dreaming is another way to think about it. It is an explosion of thought that can elicit a loud sound, laughter, and giggle from your heart. Yes, it's explosive, and you'll know when your instinct says it's right on!

Become like Walt Disney, who is my hero for demonstrating the power of imagination. Disney coined the term "Imagineers." Become your own self-appointed "imagineer." That will fuel dreams, generate thinking, inspire conversation, and generate action. And everything changes.

Your new ride can be as imaginative as anything Walt ever created.

My advice to myself is, "Dream big, Bob. Why not?"

Discussion thought-starters

What would be some examples of dreaming inside the box?
What would be some examples of dreaming outside the box?

What would be some examples of dreams that simply make you giggle with joy? "Dare to dream that you can make a difference."

— Max Lucado

"Imagination is more important than knowledge."
— Albert Einstein

"Most Americans honestly believe America is the most powerful nation on earth; but actually the most powerful nation is imagi-nation."
— Zig Ziglar

"You cannot move toward anything fulfilling if you're not dreaming."
— Bob Boylan

You cannot move toward anything fulfilling
if you're not dreaming!

The Past is Prologue

An often-quoted line from Shakespeare's *The Tempest* is "What's past is prologue."

Hopefully you are beginning to get the drift that you have an absolutely incredible opportunity in front of you to paint the picture of your future.

To design Your New Adventure!

The painter is you, not your former organization. You'll select the colors from your palette and paint what you see ahead of you as a possibility. As you paint, your past is a prologue to help you go forward in your future.

You have arrived at this point in your life having achieved what the world defines as success. In Bob Buford's book *Beyond Halftime*, he says now you have the opportunity to paint your picture of becoming "significant."

The palette from which you're choosing the colors to paint the remainder of your life's picture is your prologue. It's full of bright colors. Maybe it's got its share of dull colors. Now, as the painter, you have the opportunity to change them to a palette full of brilliant colors with which to paint the picture of your new life.

Discussion thought-starters
What are some dull colors of your past that should not be used again?
What colors should you paint now to help you become more significant?

"Instincts allow your internal vision to become an external reality."

— T.D. Jakes

You have the opportunity to paint your picture
of becoming "significant."

See Your Life through the Lens of Gratitude

The major skill landscape photographers bring to the process is our ability to "see the composition." Our ability to "see" better is what will distinguish the outcome of a great picture versus just a snapshot.

For the last fifteen years of my life I've been working diligently to see my life THROUGH the lens of gratitude.

I keep focusing on seeing what I have, instead of what I don't have. As you review your past, try looking at it in this manner. See your past through the lens of gratitude. Focus on what you have, not on what you don't have or have not achieved. Keep your singular focus on what you have in all facets of your life.

I'm confident you will "see" an exemplary past.

This past becomes your prologue to Your New Adventure!

Discussion thought-starters

Have you already been thinking this way? If you have already adopted this idea of being grateful, please share with others how that attitude has produced even more things in your life to be grateful for.

Will this concept be a big change for you?

Bob Boylan

Keep focusing on seeing what you have,
instead of what you don't have.

You've Got to be Kidding!

For more than forty-five years, I have been a practitioner of "going outside the box." My current book, *Stop Being Predictable*, has the entire content based on this principle.

This puzzle is used to teach creative thinking all over the world. Most of us live inside the box most of the time, but you now can decide to live outside the box more than you have in the past.

My long study of this principle concludes that almost all great ideas are outside the box. Venturing outside the box quickly generates two strong feelings: You're very lonely, and this feels risky.

At this stage in life, your financial base is probably large enough to allow you to take more risks because you aren't driven by economic success.

Also, at this stage of your life, you may discover that your home is larger than you need and you have more stuff than you need. This is a very common discovery. Therefore, you can go outside the box and dream about where you might rather live, and ask yourself how much stuff you really need.

My wife and I decided to listen to our hearts, sell our home and almost everything in it, and move to Austria in September 2013. We gathered friends and family around to tell them of our "faith adventure." Most of the reactions can be summarized with a one-word comment.

"Wow!," our friends would say. Also, many times it was followed by the comment, "I simply couldn't get rid of all my stuff."

The purpose of giving you this example is not to suggest that you sell your home and all your stuff; it's to show you what outside-the-box thinking is like.

We simply did not want to say, "You know, we actually would've been okay. . . . You know we could have done that. . . . Oh man, we should have done it when we thought about it!"

This entire book attempts to put forth ideas that may be just a nudge outside your box. In fact, some of your thinking and dreaming may cause you to venture quite far outside your box.

Discussion thought-starters

What are some examples of dreams for your future that would make your friends say, "You've got to be kidding!"

Obviously your spouse needs to agree just how far outside the box you should think. What are some given limitations to this line of thinking?

What are some obvious outside-the-box actions you can hardly wait to take?

What way-outside-the-box ideas are you currently considering?

What major lifestyle changes get you excited?

Connect these nine dots using just four lines . . .

What people often do looks like this:

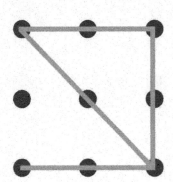

View the correct solution on the next page . . .

Correct solution: Think outside the box

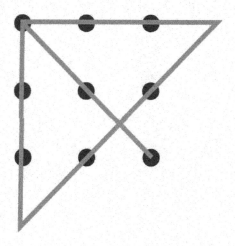

What outside the box ideas already
have you stimulated?

What If There is No Box?

When we are working, all kinds of boxes surround how we think. Some boxes have very thick lines, and we never go outside those boxes.

We are consistently told to "Think outside the box because we need fresh ideas on this problem."

Now you're transitioning into a new phase of life. You're retiring, and with that transition, maybe you can throw away the obstacle of thinking as you always have—staying inside the box most of the time, and once in awhile having the courage to go outside the lines—and be free to run outside the lines.

You can now think with more freedom, outside the lines.

You may now "see no box at all."

Your new way of seeing your life by definition will be free.

Discussion thought-starters

At least try a few ideas to see if they elicit any giggles.

Generate a few "way out" ideas and watch your friends respond with great passion, "You really have got to be kidding!"

What Size is Your Frying Pan?

Mary Morrissey, in her book *Building Your Field of Dreams,* tells this story.

There was a man fishing who kept throwing back the biggest fish he caught.

A guy who was fishing next to him broke the silence. "Gosh, I've been watching you fish all afternoon, and that was the biggest fish you caught. I don't get it. Why did you throw it back?"

The old man responded, "Well, you see, my frying pan is only ten inches wide. Anything that doesn't fit in my pan goes back."

My thought is that your frying pan is the size of the life you have known.

Our Creator sends us fish—ideas—to nourish us, to build the life we want to live. When an idea comes that's bigger than the frying pan we *have* known, we toss it. We throw it back into the ocean of ideas, saying, "No, that won't fit, so that idea isn't for me."

God's currency is ideas. The people who realize their dreams are the ones who are careful not to discard ideas that can nourish them and lead them to a more abundant life.

Therefore, design the biggest frying pan you've ever seen. See that it is large enough to hold any of your new ideas.

Make it large enough to hold the biggest "catch" of your life.

Discussion thought-starters

I believe the frying pan of your current life may be too small. Do you agree?

What initial ideas about the next steps of your life necessitate increasing the size of your frying pan?

By not increasing the size of your frying pan, I believe you are deciding to mostly gear down. Does that feel comfortable to you, or limiting?

"What single step could you take to minimize the regret factor at the end of your life?"

— John Ortberg

Do you need a bigger frying pan?

Petrified Opinion Halts Dreams

As you share with friends and family your outside-the-box ideas, some of the ideas will be attacked. They will look at you with great sincerity in their eyes and voice and say, "You've got to be kidding!"

Your good friends are trying to protect you from getting hurt.

But it is their petrified opinion of what is a reasonable dream for you that can put a screeching halt to your dream.

Don't allow their petrified opinions to keep you inside the box.

Discussion thought-starters
Decide what will help you move forward with your thinking, and who will have a tendency to always put the brakes on.

Open the Door

Theophane was a monk who lived in St. Benedict's Monastery in Snowmass, Colorado. The monastery was our neighbor at the time. Through the years, Theophane became a very close friend and wise counselor.

In his book *Tales of the Magic Monastery*, he tells the story of a man who walked by the door of a beautiful building, knowing that inside was peace, joy, and happiness.

He writes that the man did not feel worthy to open the door even though he knew what was inside. One day he worked up his courage and opened the door. And yes, from that time on, he lived with peace, joy, and happiness.

As you define the options that will guide Your New Adventure, don't be afraid to open the door to peace, joy, and happiness.

As you think through these opportunities, the door may become clearly defined. Then all it takes is the courage to open the door and walk through.

There is mounting research on the subject that we are addressing that suggests you may be about to open the door to the most joy-filled and significant ride of your life.

Discussion thought-starters

What doors offer you the opportunity to lead a life of significance?

What doors will challenge you to gear up the most?

As we look back on our lives, what are the doors we went through, even though there were significant challenges, and what doors did we choose not to go through?

What doors offer you the opportunity
to lead a life of significance?

Where is the "WOW"?

This is a question author Tom Peters asks. He is a true master of this concept.

For years I have asked my presentation workshop participants, "Where is the WOW in your presentation?"

When you get to a senior position in your business life, you and your competition make amazingly similar presentations. Amazingly, frighteningly, predictably similar. That's why I wrote the book, *Stop Being Predictable!*

In order to differentiate yourself from your competition, you must be willing to try something new. That's not a new idea. I know you've heard this one before. But in order to differentiate, you need to go outside the box. You truly need to do something different in your presentation. That's the wow. And we all know it's difficult for people to go outside the box.

In terms of the presentation world that I've lived in for so long, your associates will say (and in my experience might say quite adamantly): "But we've always done it like this. Why would you want to do it differently?"

The basic question you're asking yourself now is, "Do I only gear down, as the picture has been painted for so many years, or do I want to both gear down and up for a better, New Adventure?"

When you tell people about what you're planning to do now that you've retired, will they say, "Wow, that's pretty amazing. That's a big idea. In fact, if that idea works, it could radically change a lot of people's lives including yours"?

Why not think that big? Why not become that courageous and imaginative?

Discussion thought-starters

As you generate your gear-up ideas," imagine telling someone about them and getting the response of: "Wow, that's an incredible idea!"

Consider a "Wow" response as a measuring stick as you discuss ideas with friends. It is a very energizing discussion of ideas!

Seriously?

This quite predictable response is heard when someone utters a fresh thought, a brand-new way of looking at solving a problem, or a brand-new way of defining an opportunity.

You hear folks say, "Seriously?"

Someone will look at you and say, "But you have never done anything like this before." Get ready for this well-intended pearl of wisdom from your closest friends and family.

It seems to be a response that questions your intellectual prowess. It gets to the heart of questioning your ability to think logically, which will deliver a predictable outcome.

What it can do, furthermore, if you allow it, is tone down your dreaming quotient. It will keep you inside the box. It's not fun having your good friends and confidants question you with this one word. But can you imagine how many times the great innovators of history heard this word? How many times did Walt Disney get questioned like this? And of course, they may have even snickered when Walt said, "Yes, seriously."

Naturally you will have done lots of homework to get the facts on the table so that your idea is not foolhardy. It's not just an idea off your right hip. However, in your opinion, this new way of looking at Your New Adventure is a serious opportunity to lead a much more exciting and significant life.

So when they say to you, "Seriously?" your answer is, "Yes, you bet I'm serious." It's possible you might even add, "Would you like to come along on this New Adventure with me?

Discussion thought-starters

Will you have the courage to dream big enough so that you can predict some people will say, "Seriously?"

Consider measuring your new ideas by how much people say, "Seriously?"

RETIREMENT: Your New Adventure

Does it excite you to be challenged by, "Seriously"?

Contribute

Ben Sandler's book *The Art of Possibility* is where this idea of contribution comes from. Focus on being a contributor. That's it. Simple. I can remember that as I go about my day: Be a contributor by really seeing what's before me, who's before me, what I am being asked to do, etc. So simple. So actionable.

A story that I use in teaching presentation workshops is from Father John Powell, who was a Jesuit priest at Loyola University in Chicago. Father Powell said that after he was out working in schools for twelve years, he was invited back to speak to his fellow 129 Jesuit priests.

He was in the "green room" before going on stage to give his presentation. He asked himself, "Why am I nervous?"

He answered his own question: "I'm nervous because I'm getting ready to perform instead of contribute."

In my job as a presentation trainer, I tell workshop participants this story because when we make a presentation, the purpose is not to perform but to contribute. The only reason we are presenting is to help the listener.

New research on longevity says people who are contributing to others, giving their services away on a volunteer basis, live longer.

My mentor Jim Shannon said to me, "There is nothing wrong with you helping out at soup kitchens, Bob. However, you have more to contribute, so why don't you find a place where you can contribute at your highest level?"

The famous motivational speaker and author Zig Ziglar's basic concept is: "You can have everything in life you want, if you will just help enough other people get what they want."

Conceivably the core idea of Your New Adventure! is focusing on making a contribution.

Discussion thought-starters

How can your gifts be contributed? Discuss the significant impact your contributions of time and talent can make.

Discuss if this measuring stick, the impact of your contributions, will be the major criterion to help you decide how you will design Your New Adventure!

"You can have everything in life you want, if you will just help enough other people get what they want."
— Zig Ziglar

The Key to Happiness

In Gail Sheehy's book Passages, she writes that she came across an incredibly lucky group of people she called "people of high well-being" that made her intensely curious. "How," she asked, "had they achieved such a state of fulfillment and happiness?"

She was really asking the question: "What is the key to happiness?"

She discovered they had seven things in common.

One of the seven things was this: They had all taken a very significant risk in their lives.

My thought is that it is only by risking . . . that we really live life at all.

The essence of going outside the box has at its heart the courage to take a risk.

Discussion thought-starters

What big risks are you willing to consider?

Do you see how taking risks would generate tremendous adventure in your life, even if the ideas don't work?

Or do you feel much more comfortable not taking risks at this stage?

What big risks are you willing to consider?

Who's Responsible Now?

I mentioned mirrors in chapter one with the idea that the windshield is bigger than the rearview mirror. But mirrors can also be useful. Even big mirrors.

One reason I have enjoyed a self-employed career is that when something is not working right, I just need to look in the mirror. What I see is the person who needs to fix the problem. Quite possibly, what I see is the person who is the problem. I don't need any committee meetings or anybody giving me a performance review.

I simply look in the mirror.

It's similar for you now. Look in the mirror because you are responsible for the rest of your life.

Unlike baseball, there are no designated hitters.

No one can take your place.

Maybe it's time to put a new, larger mirror in your home so that when you walk by it, you can continually remind yourself that who you're looking at is responsible for the life you are living.

Discussion thought-starters

There are no designated hitters in this situation. Are you up for this 100 percent responsibility?

Does this idea get you charged up?

What limitations that have been in place on how you have been living your life can now be discarded?

Your GPS

We all have our own guidance system.

It has been built through your education and life experiences.

My own guidance system is I have always had God in the passenger seat riding along with me. He's always been there, and I have leaned on Him heavily.

However, I finally decided to let God drive the car. I have finally decided to trust him 100 percent.

Therefore, God is my GPS.

Discussion thought-starters

Is this a good time to adjust, possibly even reconsider, just what does guide you?

We learned to depend on our GPS to arrive at the right location. The deeper question is, "What is your own GPS system?"

Stop Rehearsing Potential Disaster

It's frighteningly easy to get caught in this trap.

You begin by thinking about a small problem you actually have. Then you start to magnify that problem by telling yourself, if such and such happened, then this would probably happen.

And if that happened, this would probably happen. And if that happened . . . on and on until you have worked yourself into a frenzy.

You have succeeded in focusing on potential disasters. You know it's not the correct way of thinking, but you've just done it again.

I can't tell you how many times I've gone into that downward spiral. I eventually catch myself and say, "It's the words I use that determine what happens. Stop saying these things, Bob!"

Hopefully you are deep into the process of saying things you want to have happen. Do not allow yourself to get caught in a downward spiral of focusing on potential disaster if the things don't happen per your plan.

The best bumper sticker I ever saw said, "Life happens on plan B."

Focus on outcome, not process. Sometimes we may choose the wrong process while attempting to reach the outcome we dream about. Then it's possible we start in a downward spiral of focusing on potential disaster because the process is not working correctly.

Regroup by rethinking, and create a new process based on the outcome you desire.

Discussion thought-starters

Do you have a history of allowing your focus on potential disaster derail you as you strive for your goals?

Since this is an easy habit to fall into, what might you do to learn to focus on outcome, not Process?

"Focus on outcome, not process."

Get Noticed

Human resource professionals say that the most important thing all of us want is to be recognized. To be noticed.

We all have experienced walking into a room and feeling that no one saw us. We weren't noticed at all. It was like we were not even there. It was a terrible feeling.

The idea here is that we all want to be noticed.

This is your chance to really be noticed. You have the opportunity to script how you're noticed. How you are described. How you are recognized. How you are talked about. How you will be remembered.

Passionately contribute more of yourself to help others.

This always gets noticed.

Discussion thought-starters

How can you use your gifts to set yourself apart?

Where can you contribute the most, and be remembered for that?

Passionately contribute more of yourself to help others.

Measurable Progress

For whom did I do something? What did I do? How much of it did I do? All of these are measurable aspects that we were so used to in our normal workflow while we were working.

I personally have the need to feel productive each day. This act of contribution is so simple that I can start each day by saying, "What can I intentionally contribute to a person, an organization, my community, a friend, etc?"

Then I go looking for the opportunity to do it.

I have a bias towards action. Towards "getting on with it." I really like the Nike slogan, "Just Do It" I hope you find in this book ideas and simple concepts that you will act on.

"Just do it." Three words. That simple three-word sentence is all over the world. Maybe it's your time to simply mimic that and move out with gusto.

Maybe you're like me and also want some sort of measurable progress every day.

I like the idea of focusing on contributing because I can actually journal what I contributed today.

Discussion thought-starters
What can I intentionally contribute to a person, an organization, my community, or a friend that is measurable?
Measurability is something you are used to in your professional life. Discuss how measurability lets you know you are making progress.

"Progress involves risks; you can't steal second base and keep your foot on first."
— Frederick Wilcox

We Become What We Think About

Every major philosopher, self-image psychologist, and intellectual Bible teacher agree on this single idea.

- We become what we think about.
- We become our most dominant thought.
- The Bible says, "As a man thinketh, so is he."

Therefore, we should pay attention to what we're thinking about. Many thoughts come into our minds unasked for. It happens frequently throughout the day. We need a process to get rid of the thoughts we don't want so that we can focus on the productive ones.

Some years ago, pastor Mark Bintliff of New Creation Church in Glenwood Springs, Colorado, had a series of sermons on the question, "What's on your mind?" The idea was to come up with something that you could refer to often that would quickly direct your mind into thinking about what is proper and life-giving.

It helps eliminate all of the clutter that tends to inappropriately fill my mind.

I created the following prayer. I actually say the following words out loud three times a day. I picture God talking to me, and He says: "Bob, I want you to lead a passionate, purposeful, diligent, hopeful, joyful, courageous, and worry-free life. Trust Me 100 percent because I have it all figured out. Be at peace and don't worry. And Bob, it's going to be so great, you won't even believe it."

I have been saying that daily for many years. I simply know it helps focus my thinking. I know those words motivate and console me.

It is a forceful directive to jolt me into getting the right things on my mind.

What can you create that you can say repetitively to help you answer the question, "What's on your mind?"

"We become what we think about." Being aware of the significance of this sequence helps me focus on the right things.

Discussion thought-starters

Create gearing-up ideas that are easy to think about.

These ideas will eventually be the core of your "purpose statement."

You Will Talk About Something

Lou Tice, a self-image psychologist in Seattle, Washington, created the idea called "Self-Talk."

He says we talk to ourselves at eight hundred words per minute. In fact, we cannot stop talking to ourselves, so therefore, we need to understand how important what we say to ourselves really is.

Therefore, proactively decide what your conversation with yourself will be all about.

I believe it all starts with dreaming. I like to say:

- What we dream about, we think about.
- What we think about, we talk about.
- What we talk about with some repetition, we act on.
- What we act on regularly becomes a habit.
- Our habits generate our character.

Our character determines our destiny.
I have found this to be true.

- What we dream about, we think about.
- What we think about, we begin talking about.
- And if you can't say it, you'll never have it!

Discussion thought-starters

As you dialogue with yourself and others, what new, fresh opportunities naturally excite you that you find yourself talking about a great deal?

If you can talk about them with clarity and passion, they simply will not happen.

If you cannot talk about them with clarity, they won't happen.

"In all of your ways acknowledge Him, and He will direct your paths."

— Proverbs 3:6

Redirecting

Here are different words that I believe redirecting means. Pick the one that resonates and best describes how you feel about Your New Adventure!

Re-firing

Re-deploying

Re-engineering

Remodeling

Revitalizing

Renewing

Rebuilding

Reconsidering

Discussion thought-starters

Decide which word conveys to yourself and others the way you think and what you will talk about.

Which word describes, in general, how you see yourself gearing up?

Airplanes

Are you coming in for a soft landing, or are you taking off?

For decades you have been picturing retirement. That picture many times includes a couple sitting on their sundrenched patio, two glasses of orange juice on the table, a steaming hot cup of coffee, and some fruit. There is a blurred-out picture of a golf course in the background and the advertiser's name, which is, many times, a wealth management company.

These are all good things. We need to have our financial ducks in a row in order to retire comfortably. We need vendors that help us manage our assets and make prudent decisions as we downsize. How long will our asset base last is the core question.

However, I claim, it's your choice!

You can focus on coming in for a soft landing: lots of travel, lots of golf, lots of getting together with your buddies and talking about the good old times.

Or you can begin to think of Your New Adventure in life as a bundle of opportunities to be significant.

- To contribute.
- To leave a legacy.
- And also to enjoy Your New Adventure!

Webster's dictionary defines "opportunity" as a set of circumstances that makes it possible to do something. But you must "see" that set of circumstances clearly to picture your opportunity. You must see the set of circumstances that are created by your retirement as positive.

Discussion thought-starters
Are you planning to come in for a soft landing, or are you taking off? Both are valid, and you will talk with passion about the New Adventure you have chosen.

Which New Adventure gets you most excited?

Which New Adventure will you naturally talk about with energy?

"Your mission, should you choose to accept it..."
— Mission: Impossible TV series

"If you can't see it, you can't say it. If you can't say it, you'll never have it."
— Bob Boylan

Expectation to Flourish

"When you flourish, you become more you. You become You-ier."

— John Ortberg

The dictionary defines flourish as "to grow luxuriantly; to thrive; to achieve success; to prosper; to be in a state of activity or production; to reach a height of development or influence."

My wife and I's plan for this year has a very bold title:

"EXPECTATION TO FLOURISH. AGAIN!"

We believe in the power of very specific visioning. Not a general wish or desire, but exactly what we see in our future. This type of visioning is all backed up with lots of research and experiential evidence, and it works in spades.

It has been working for us. We expect it to continue working for us.

As you are nearing the end of this book, it is legitimate to ask yourself these very basic questions:

What are your specific expectations? What will happen quite specifically on this adventure you are designing? As we all know, it's the adventure that is the joy of life.

Discussion thought-starters

How would you explain the feelings you have about deciding to go on this new adventure?

How would you describe your feelings about the adventure not being successful?

"The indispensable first step to getting the things you want out of life is this: Decide what you want."

— Brian Tracy

Trust ME, Just Jump!

Our pastor at New Creation Church in Glenwood Springs, Colorado was Mark Bintliff.

One Sunday pastor Mark was role-playing his experience of standing in a swimming pool with his arms outstretched to his little daughter who was standing on the deck of the pool.

He was pleading with her and saying, "Trust me honey, just jump." And of course, the daughter answered in a frightened voice, "But Daddy, I'm bigger now. Can you really catch me?"

"Yes, honey, trust me. Just jump."

You may have this feeling as you enter into designing Your New Adventure! Your new adventure may be dramatically different from what you have been doing, dramatically different than what you thought you might be doing, and dramatically different from what other people would have predicted you would do upon retirement.

But you feel you just have to jump.

Since we have a very strong faith, I write this sentence this way.

"Trust ME, just jump."

Discussion thought-starters

Common sense will guide just how far you jump in terms of your financial resources. Discuss your fears in making such a large jump.

Decide if your large jump creates enough joy and expectation to be worth the risk.

Even if the jump doesn't succeed, is it still worth jumping?

"Life is not about the breaths you take. It's about the moments that take your breath away."

— Anonymous

If You Want to Win

Lou Holtz, the famous football coach, tells the story of asking his players if their desire to win is strong enough for the team to become number one.

He reminds them that the only way to become number one is to do all the necessary work diligently and with perseverance. That will give them the chance to win and possibly become number one.

You know the picture. They are standing there, jumping up and down with their index finger pointed to the sky saying, "You bet we want to win! You bet we want to be number one!"

Lou says, "Okay. If you really want to win, you need to understand what those letters, WIN, stand for. They stand for: What's Important Now."

Your job is to decide what is important now as you visualize your next adventure through life. As I send you to the drawing boards, many of these ideas are BGOs. I hope some are fresh thoughts to assist you in making the best choice you can to design Your New Adventure!

Discussion thought-starters

All great plans degenerate into work.

So what is the first thing you would go to work on? What's important now?

Nike has a wonderful saying: "Just Do It."

There's No Hiding from Deciding

You're about to leave work and professional life as you've known it. There are no designated hitters to make this decision for you. There is no hiding from the deciding.

"Ready or not, here I come!"

Remember the playground game called hide and seek?

Everyone was running to hide someplace, and you were standing still with your eyes closed.

Then you shout at the top of your lungs, "Ready or not, here I come!"

Make sure you plan to be ready.

Your Expanded Life Plan

I hope your expanded life plan has a "WOW" response when your friends and family hear about it. You will smile, and your smile will be infectious!

A good friend of mine taught goal-setting as a consultant for more than thirty years. He knew a lot about goals. The one fact he told me that never can be erased from my memory: 80 percent of written plans are attained. "If they're not written, good luck."

With that piece of evidence, why would we not create a written whole-life plan?

I've been doing this whole-life planning since 1987, writing what I call "My Expanded Life Plan." Every year I write one, I think of my former mentor Jim Shannon's wisdom in coming up with that title.

One year I had written a plan called "My Slow-Down Plan." He looked at me and said, "Very good thinking, Bob. Very detailed and well-thought-out. But you have the wrong title."

We got into some pretty heated discussion about why I thought the title was correct.

He listened and then said, "You don't get it, do you? This is your expanded life plan, Bob. You are not slowing down, Bob. You are expanding your life. Don't you see that?"

Writing "My Expanded Life Plan" each year has been one of the most powerful habits I have ever established. It has allowed me to live an abundant life; a victorious life; an ever-expanding life. And, I believe, a very productive life.

It's possible that you now have a great opportunity to execute this concept because you are no longer burdened with your former professional life's never-ending new initiatives.

Now you have the time and a strong rationale to write your whole-life plan. And with that fact, it has a very good chance of becoming reality. By the way, title it appropriately.

Discussion thought-starters

Is this the first time you've ever written this type of a plan, instead of just your professional life plan? In your professional life, it was normal to have written an annual plan. You believed in it. It was part of what you did on a regular basis because it was valuable.

The same thing is true now, but you are committing to paper an annual plan for your entire life.

Discuss with others how exciting this should be.

"Does your calendar reflect your passion?"
— Max Lucado

"NOW your calendar can reflect your passion."
— Bob Boylan

NOW your calendar can reflect your passion.

Your Final Performance Review

I believe when I pass away and I'm sitting before God, I will experience my final performance review.

I can picture God saying, "I gave you a number of talents and skills. What have you done with those gifts? Of course, I do know what you've done, but I would like to hear it in your own words, Bob."

John Ortberg, author of many books, tells the story like this.

On your tombstone will be a year you were born, a dash (–), and the year you die. You have no control over those years. HOWEVER, you have a great deal of control over the –.

The dash represents what you will talk about in your final performance review. It's your next adventure now. That adventure will put more into your dash.

Discussion thought-starters

You are used to annual performance reviews. Now, on your final performance review, what do you want to talk most about?

Why does that get you excited?

You are at a point where you are now able to decide what you will talk most about.

"It's not what you know or who you know. It's what you are that finally counts."

— Zig Ziglar

BOB BOYLAN

ABOUT THE AUTHOR

Bob Boylan lives his life based on these foundational principles:

The glory of God is a human being "fully alive"!

Do not lead a woulda, coulda, shoulda life.

Holy Spirit is Bob's best friend, shepherd, chief operating officer and strategic partner.

Bob and his wife, Linda, live in Woodland Park, Colorado.

www. Bobboylan.com

It's My Pleasure

Offer from the author

I have deep longings in my heart, to try and help people understand they have an opportunity for a new adventure in their retirement.

You can call me free of charge at 719-417-4755, to discuss ideas or questions you have.

As mentioned in the book, I am a "seed planter of ideas to creatively encourage and inspire others."

It's possible, we might have quite an energized conversation!

When you call, you'll be asked to leave your name, phone number and email.

I'm looking forward to being available for you.

Bob Boylan

OTHER BOOKS BY THE AUTHOR

What's Your Point?
The three-step method for making
effective presentations

Get Everyone in Your Boat
Rowing in the Same Direction
Five Leadership Principles to Follow
So Others Will Follow You

Stop Being Predictable
14 Tactics that will make Your Presentations
Insanely Effective!

"4 Ideas with actionable wisdom"
How to: Balance Your Life, Be More Grateful,
Make Changes More Effectively, Be More Creative

Retirement: Your New Adventure $14.95